Habits of Happiness

Habits of
Happiness

WENDY ULRICH, PhD

DESERET
BOOK

Salt Lake City, Utah

Visit us at DeseretBook.com

Library of Congress Cataloging-in-Publication Data

(CIP data on file)
ISBN 978-1-60907-817-1

Printed in the United States of America
R. R. Donnelley, Crawfordsville, IN

10   9   8   7   6   5   4   3   2   1

For my beautiful grandchildren

Being Happy

Happiness is the outcome divinely designed into the fabric of our very existence. It is what God intends for us. His plan for our salvation is often referred to as "the great plan of happiness" (Alma 42:8). But we don't get happiness by just deciding to be happy. We don't even get happiness by pursuing it directly. Happiness results when we get on the right path—a path of living in accordance with our highest ideals.

Recent research in the field of psychology supports the importance of living our values if we want happiness and well-being. Over most of its existence as a discipline, psychology primarily pursued the goal of helping people heal—helping people get back to neutral, if you will—when their paths had begun in painful, negative places. Then a decade or so ago a psychologist named Martin Seligman got together with some of his psychologist friends and proposed a new field of inquiry for the field of psychology: not just how people get from mental illness to neutral or zero, but how people get from zero to positive. How do people thrive, not merely survive? How do they become resilient, resourceful, and happy? Seligman got a jump-start on his project when an anonymous donor offered him $20 million to pursue his research because the donor felt so strongly about Seligman's goals.[1] That's a happy way to start a research agenda.

When Seligman began to look at what helps people to be happy, he was quickly joined by other researchers interested in what actually helps people flourish and make a difference for good in the world. They realized that happiness is not just a feeling we happen upon, but a skill set we can develop. The feeling of "I'm so happy!" may come and go, but the sense of having overall happiness in our lives can increase when we get on the right path. Some interesting ideas have come out of that research, many of which are consistent with the gospel of Jesus Christ, although it may not look that way right off the bat. Let's look at some habits of happiness, most of which come out of the extensive research of Seligman and his colleagues. They are:

1. Stop worrying about your weaknesses.
2. Don't even try to get motivated to exercise.
3. Stop hoping to find friends.
4. Don't try to feel happier.
5. Celebrate failure.
6. Don't try to get help with your problems.
7. Don't endure to the end.

Now, maybe you read that list and think, "Somebody just wasted $20 million." Or maybe you think, "If Wendy can get away with promoting a list like that at Deseret Book, then this is the church for me!" Before you get too excited either way, let's take a closer look at this counterintuitive list of some of the habits of happiness.

1. Don't Worry about Your Weaknesses

With all the emphasis in the scriptures on repentance, worrying about our weaknesses has almost become a national pastime for good Christian folk and Latter-day Saints in particular. One of the first things Seligman figured out was that we don't necessarily get happier by trying to fix what's wrong with us. Fixing what's wrong gets us to neutral, to being less miserable and having more options. But we are more likely to get to the positive side, to happiness, by pursuing our strengths.[2] So this first habit should really be titled: "Put most of your energy into contributing to the world from your strengths, not into overcoming your weaknesses."

That's kind of an interesting lesson for those of us who spend a lot of time thinking about what's wrong with us. Trying to get better at what we're lousy at is still a good thing to do, of course, especially when it includes repenting of genuine sin. But it's not necessarily what makes for happiness in the day-to-day living of our lives. We are more likely to be happy when we develop and live from our strengths, put our highest values into action, and do what we love.

It's not too hard for me to imagine that the Lord is pleased when we focus on contributing to the world from our strengths rather than get bogged down in a self-focused preoccupation with our weaknesses. I decided a few months ago to review my patriarchal blessing, wanting to better understand what the Lord wants me to be doing with my life. Just for fun, I decided to make a list of what things He told me were potential strengths and what things He told me were potential weaknesses. It was quite interesting to make those lists. I assumed going in, although I wasn't really conscious of it, that the *weaknesses* list would be quite long. I thought I would find a lot of warnings and things I really needed to buck up and fix—and I assumed that if I could figure out what was wrong with me and fix it, I'd feel better. But I actually found only about five instances of that kind of thing, and some of those I had to stretch to include. (For example, my blessing said something about me being humble, and I thought maybe that was an indirect way of telling me to be careful about pride, so I put "pride" on the *weaknesses* list.)

In contrast, I found more than forty things in this little one-page document about my gifts, my opportunities, and my strengths. I don't think I'm unusual here. You might review your patriarchal blessing with a similar purpose. There seems to be something foundational about the importance of working on our strengths as a guide to life.

I learned something about this principle when my husband and I served a mission a few years ago in Quebec, Canada. I served a mission when I was younger as well, and I had some regrets about not having been the best missionary possible on that first mission. I hadn't done anything horrible, but I wasn't perfect at living all the rules and I wasn't always very enthusiastic about every single aspect of missionary work. So when we went on this new mission, I was determined to overcome those early deficits. I made a list of things I needed to work on, and it was a very, very long list. For openers, I am just not a natural missionary by any stretch of the imagination, and talking to strangers about the gospel is really hard for me, as I know it is for many. I practiced and I tried and I worked, but I wasn't very successful and I wasn't very happy. In addition, I felt like a terrible hypocrite because I was supposed to be an example and even a trainer for the younger missionaries in how to effectively share the gospel, be more in tune with the Spirit, and obey mission rules. Some of those things came naturally to me, but some absolutely did not. In fact, it felt like the harder I tried at some things, the more miserable I became.

One night I was in my office moaning to the Lord about all these weaknesses that I felt made me completely inadequate in the calling we were trying to serve in. I was literally lying on the floor crying, telling the Lord I didn't belong there. And the Spirit came through loud and clear, even though it came as a whisper: "Wendy, I didn't call you here for your weaknesses, I called you for your strengths."

A light went on in my head. The idea that God wants us to magnify our gifts—as opposed to magnifying our inadequacies—was not a new one for me, but suddenly it was personal, present, and real. I started thinking about some of the strengths I had that I could bring to the mission. I was the first mission president's wife in that mission in many decades who spoke French, the language of most of the people. I was reasonably comfortable speaking in large groups. I was a psychologist by training. I had served a full-time mission. I *loved* the missionaries and deeply understood their frustrations and fears. I had spent a lifetime studying and teaching the gospel. In other words, I had many strengths I could bring to the missionaries and to the mission field. And here I had been putting so much of my energy into fretting about my weaknesses! I was so worried about bringing my weaknesses to neutral, to zero, that I forgot about the positive side of the scale—the path that gets us to happy. I found more courage and energy to keep working on my weaknesses when I focused more on contributing from my strengths.

Interestingly, Seligman, who is not a religious man

himself (or, by his own admission, a particularly happy person), began his research on human happiness by combing the great religions of the world for the collective wisdom of humanity about the good life. As he looked for the positive traits that humanity universally values, he came up with the following list of "signature strengths" people might acquire. [3] As you read over this list, find two or three things you really want to be known for—things you value and exhibit in your life. Or look for two or three things that your mother or best friend would say are your qualities if she were introducing you to someone. If you want a more scientific and systematic way of figuring out what your character virtues or

Focus on your strengths, not your weaknesses.

strengths are, go to the website www.authentichappi-ness.com, which is Seligman's research site, and you will find several free tests that will give a little more detailed look at your strengths.

A quick hint: This book is filled with little exercises that you'll benefit most from if you write some things down. You'll see a few lines that you can jot down a couple of thoughts on, but the best idea would be to get yourself a notebook, or pull up a new document on your computer or other electronic device, and do the writing exercises there.

Signature Strengths

- Curiosity
- Love of learning
- Open-mindedness
- Creativity
- Seeing the big picture
- Bravery
- Persistence
- Honesty and authenticity
- Enthusiasm
- Self-discipline
- Caution

- Forgiveness
- Humility, modesty
- Kindness and generosity
- Social skill to fit in, connect
- Loving and accepting love
- Being a team player
- Fairness to all
- Leadership
- Appreciating beauty or excellence
- Gratitude for others
- Humor and playfulness
- Religiousness or spirituality
- Optimism[4]

What are two or three of these "signature strengths" that you especially value?

_____

_____

Happiness researchers find that if people use one or more of their strengths or virtues in a new and creative way, they typically see a small boost in their feelings of well-being and happiness. If they keep that up, finding more new and creative ways to live their highest values each week, they continue to feel a little better overall.[5]

For example, if one of your signature strengths is "religiousness or spirituality," a new and creative way to use that strength this week might be to go outside and look at the stars, contemplating your relationship with their Creator, if that is not something you generally do. Or perhaps you would enjoy learning how to meditate, developing a new format to keep track of lessons you learn from the scriptures, writing down an experience this week that deepened your sense of the meaning of life, reviewing general conference talks for ways to develop spiritually, putting extra creativity into your Church calling, or sharing your feelings about God with a coworker.

Now, make a list of some of your other personal strengths:

- What are two or three of your personal talents— things that come naturally to you, or talents you've developed?

_____

_____

- What are a couple of skills you've developed in the past or use regularly?

_____

_____

- What are some of the responsibilities or obligations you have this week, in particular involving other people?

_____

_____

- What opportunities are coming up for you?

_____

_____

Now look for ways to use your talents, skills, responsibilities, and opportunities—things you do every day—in ways that express the signature strengths you identified above. For example, if your signature strengths are curiosity, forgiveness, humility, bravery, and playfulness, how could you use your signature strength of curiosity to express or develop your talents, or how could you use one of your skills to better express forgiveness? How could you express humility in your relationships, display more bravery in an existing responsibility, or use playfulness to infuse an upcoming opportunity with new life? Applying our signature strengths to our daily tasks, relationships, work, and routines helps us feel the importance of our personal contributions, and we become happier about our daily lives.

Our sense of well-being will increase even more as we use our strengths to strengthen others. Humans define moral good in terms of the impact of an action on other people. Signature strengths that positively affect other people have the biggest positive impact on us as well.

What are some new and creative ways you could use one of the signature strengths you identified above to strengthen others, to fire up enthusiasm for a project, or to express your talents or interests in the coming week? Take a moment to brainstorm, or invite a friend to help you. You may or may not decide to actually do any of these, but have fun thinking up some possibilities.

_____

_____

2. Don't Try to Get Motivated to Exercise

I assume there's nobody left in the civilized world who hasn't heard that exercise will help us be healthier. But research is also pretty clear that it will help us be happier. In fact, research suggests that regular exercise will help as much as antidepressant medication if we're dealing with mild to moderate depression or anxiety.[6] I've even known people with severe depression who've tried every medication under the sun who found rigorous, daily exercise to be the only thing that really helped them feel better.

The only trouble is that about half of us hate exercise. I am one of them. Half of us can get on a treadmill, even after a little resistance, and if asked how we're feeling will say, "This feels pretty good. I'll feel better today for exercising." The other half of us would say, "I hate this. When can I stop?" We just don't like it. But whether you're in the first group or the second, regular, consistent exercise still helps you feel better overall.[7]

I know. It's tragic.

So what can you do? Many of us sit around waiting to magically get motivated to exercise. And it turns out that waiting around trying to get motivated to do something—not just exercise but anything—is a very bad idea. It almost never works. That's why this habit reads "Don't try to get motivated to exercise." If you wait until you feel motivated, you'll wait a very long time, and the benefits of exercise will elude you.

This is what to do instead. Despite your utter lack of motivation, start by doing the smallest thing you can get yourself to do that moves you even vaguely in the right direction. You get yourself in motion. And once you get moving, motivation follows.

I learned a little about this one day from (drum roll, please . . .) reading a running magazine. Yes, that's right: I was reading a running magazine. I would love you to think, "Oh, wow, Wendy reads running magazines." But of course, I *never* read running magazines. I was only reading a running magazine because I was in the chiropractor's office, he was behind, this running magazine was the *only* thing in the room to read, and I was *that* bored. Anyway, I came across this article by some guy who said he had trouble getting himself motivated to exercise. That got my attention. *I* have trouble getting myself motivated to exercise! He said, "I feel like I have these little gremlins in my brain that resist activity and extra exertion at all costs." Wow! *I* have those same gremlins in my brain!

He had a really creative way for conquering those gremlins that I've

Get moving, and the motivation will follow.

since found in several other settings online and in other books. Here's how it works: Say you're trying to create a habit of going running in the evenings. But the gremlins seem to be particularly good at talking you out of it: It's too late, you need to finish just this one thing first, you're too tired, you have to be up early tomorrow, you don't want to get yourself all stirred up before bedtime. Don't grit your teeth and fight back. Just put on your running clothes, *not because you're going running,* but because they're comfortable. Then you find a reason to go out the door, *not because you're going running,* but to check the mail or pick up a piece of trash you saw on the lawn or something. And once you're that far into it, the gremlins just give in and stop protesting, and off you go for your run.

I have tried it and found that this process actually helped. If I can do something very, very, very small to get myself started, maybe just walk down to the mailbox and back, then that is where I start. If I can give myself permission to start *that* small and *that* slow, I get past the gremlins. I start to get more motivated.

A colleague had a client whose life was so stressful and overbooked that the thought of adding exercise completely overwhelmed her. She watched half an hour of TV a day, her only relaxation, which she wasn't about to give it up. My colleague asked her to march in place for one minute during one of the commercials. One minute! She thought, "I can do that." So that was all she did for one month—one minute of marching in place. After that, she thought, "I could actually march through all the commercials." So she did that. And by the time three or four months went by, of her own free will and choice, she had gotten past the gremlins and she was marching in place for the entire thirty-minute show, which is excellent exercise.

If you need to break it down to something even smaller, do so. I know one woman who decided the only thing she could tolerate, the only thing she could slip past those gremlins, was to stand on the treadmill for two minutes while she read the newspaper. That was all she could get herself to do, but she did it, every day. Then eventually she thought, "All right, maybe I could just walk really slowly for a minute." Eventually that minute turned into a reasonable amount of steady walking.

The bottom line is, if we will just give ourselves

permission to start small enough so that we get past the gremlins of resistance, and then do that small thing often—every day—eventually the chances are good that we will decide to do a little bit more. This doesn't feel very heroic, but it is a much better plan than my previous approach to exercise, which was to start cold with ten minutes of straight running in an old pair of shoes, completely exhaust myself, end up with shin splints, and then decide to never do it again.

Motivation follows action, whether in getting yourself to exercise, clean your desk, read your scriptures, or anything else.[8] Doing any of these things for just a few minutes a day will help you feel good just because you'll feel more in control of your life and you'll stop procrastinating important or annoying tasks. But exercise will also help change the chemistry of your body and brain in a positive direction.

If you don't exercise for at least thirty minutes most days, what is one tiny step you could take in the right direction? Describe it here or in your notebook.

_____

_____

Check in with the gremlins, and make sure your goal is truly small enough to be absolutely doable, even when you have no motivation at all. Don't worry if it isn't very ambitious. Remember: motivation follows action. Get in motion, even a small motion, and see what happens over time as you persist. Eventually you'll find yourself motivated to do a little more, and the benefits of exercise on your health and happiness will follow.

3. Stop Hoping to Find Friends

If you were a manager in a company and you could start a program among your employees that had the following results, would you be interested? After this program, your employees would:

- be seven times more likely to be highly satisfied with their work than those who don't participate in the program
- be twice as likely to be satisfied with their pay, even more if they are among the lowest paid people in the organization
- miss work less often than those who don't do the program
- show more innovation and creativity

- share ideas with coworkers more
- have fewer accidents at work

Would you be interested in this program, especially if it cost almost nothing to implement? Can you guess what this "program" entails?

Actually it isn't a program at all. These are simply the outcomes the Gallup Organization found people experience when they have a best friend at work.[9] When people who have a close friend at work are compared with people who do not, those with a close friend are more satisfied with their jobs, more creative, less likely to miss work, even safer on the job. That is the power of meaningful relationships in our lives.

Can you imagine what it would do for our wards and our communities if everyone had a best friend at church, if everyone had a best friend on the block? It changes the way we feel about the world when we are connected with the people around us.

So why does this habit read, "Stop hoping to find friends?" Because sitting around hoping and waiting for someone to discover you as a friend is not a very effective strategy, in the workplace or out. A more effective strategy, one you have more control over, is to learn and practice the skills of being a friend. Let's look at some of the basic skills of friendship that researchers have found make a difference in our relationship success.

The first and most basic relationship skill, according to marital researcher John Gottman, is making bids.[10] He defines making a bid as inviting someone to pay attention to you for a moment: smiling, catching someone's eye, asking a question, using someone's name, being interested in what's going on in someone's life, paying a compliment, or starting a little conversation. That's it. Easy.

Gottman found that even in marriage, a lot of people aren't very good at making bids, however, and even more of us are not very responsive when other people make bids to us. This most basic element of human interaction is often missing even in our families, where we tend to ignore our spouses and kids as we get busy, gravitate to the computer, or get caught up in the TV. We don't think to make simple bids for involvement, and we don't really listen or respond to others. Strangers will generally make only *one* bid before giving up unless the bid is responded to positively. Family members may try harder, but having any bid ignored is still hurtful and damages relationships.

Thinking back on today or this week, how willing were you to initiate a bid in your family, your ward, your work, or your community? How attuned were you to others who made bids to you?

Bids are only the beginning of meaningful relationships, of course. To really feel heard, known, and cared about, we must be willing not only to make and respond to bids but to deepen the conversation through extended listening and sharing. If talking doesn't always come naturally to you, consider making a goal to have one truly meaningful conversation every day. If you are more of a talker, your goal might be to invest in really listening to and being curious about another person at least once a day. If you tend to keep to yourself, your goal might be to volunteer what you are honestly thinking and feeling at least once a day. Honest, meaningful conversations not only build friendships but help us learn more from our daily experience.

Gottman's research on marital relationships has also identified some relationship styles that are toxic to any relationship, whether with friends, family members, or coworkers. He learned to predict with over 90 percent accuracy whether a couple would divorce in five years based on a fifteen-minute video of the couple interacting around a relationship conflict.[11] How would you like to sign up for that video? Researchers identified four approaches that were highly predictive of divorce: criticism (pointing out faults and blaming), contempt (sarcasm, name calling, eye rolling, belittling, or other signs of disgust or disrespect), defensiveness (not owning problems, not apologizing, becoming rigid and unyielding), and stonewalling (turning away, ignoring, not sharing thoughts or feelings, changing the subject). The more of these elements, the more likely was divorce.

In contrast, people whose relationships succeed are more likely—even in the face of conflict—to remain calm, curious about the other person's thoughts and experiences, and compassionate with the other's feelings. Learning to be calm, curious, and compassionate will help us be more trustworthy friends, parents, and coworkers as well as spouses.

Another skill that helps relationships flourish is a willingness to celebrate each other's successes, including the smallest bits of good news that show up in our daily lives. Unless we pay attention, many of us tend to point out little negative things about good news, throw cold water on others' happy events, ignore the good news, or quip "That's nice, dear" without a lot of gusto. A better approach is to enthusiastically ask questions about exactly what happened— allowing the person to relive the positive experience—then offer encouragement and share in the positive emotion.[12]

Relationships also need to make room for private time, personal projects, and individual experience. There is a natural flow to a healthy relationship that swings between

Celebrate each other's successes.

connection and independence. Without separate experiences and ideas, there just isn't much to talk about, conversations become flat, one partner ends up feeling needy and ignored, and people become less interesting to each other. Relationships also benefit from *doing* things together (working on projects together or having experiences together) as well as from talking together.

All of us can practice taking the risk to make a few more bids, being more alert to the bids others make to us, toning down our tendencies to be critical, contemptuous, defensive, or stonewalling, beefing up our ability to be calm, curious, and compassionate (especially in the face of conflict), being more genuinely enthusiastic and celebratory when others have good news or success, and making space for individual goals and agendas.

Take a moment to think about your own relationship strengths and weaknesses by rating yourself on these skills (1 = I stink at this, 7 = I'm really strong in this area):

    ____ I regularly make many kinds of bids for connection and involvement.

____ I notice and respond positively and kindly to others' bids.

____ I avoid criticizing or blaming others when problems come up.

____ I don't become contemptuous, patronizing, or disrespectful, even during conflicts.

____ I don't get defensive (angry, silent, or tearful) when someone disagrees with me.

____ I don't ignore conflicts, refuse to talk about them, or withhold my thoughts.

____ I remain calm, curious about the other person, and compassionate with their feelings, even when there is a disagreement.

____ I enthusiastically celebrate others' successes or good news.

____ I have individual interests and projects, and I give my friends and family members space and support to pursue their own thoughts, interests, and goals.

After rating yourself on these skills, you might rank the two or three most important skills for you to develop, or ask a friend or family member to rate you as well. To practice these and other relationship skills, make a goal to work on one at a time until you see noticeable improvement. As you increase your relationship skills, you won't need to wait for friendship to find you. You will have the skills to create meaningful relationships that will make your workplace, ward, community, and family more satisfying, supportive, and life-enhancing.

4. Don't Try to Be Happy

I think my father fell in love with my mother because of her beautiful smile. I wasn't so blessed. I was self-conscious about the gap between my two front teeth, and I learned to hide it by smiling without parting my lips (if I smiled at all). Or perhaps I was just a grumpy child. In any case, I got an oft-repeated message from my father to *SMILE!* This always felt like being commanded to *BE HAPPY!*—which didn't feel particularly helpful.

I can gratefully report that telling others or ourselves to just *be happy* doesn't, in fact, do much of anything to lift moods. People, including children, don't turn happiness on or off as an act of will (and adding *or I'll give you something to be unhappy about* only makes things worse).

But there is a positive emotion we can access readily, which in turn will increase our feelings of happiness. That emotion is gratitude. Gratitude is always within our grasp, and research on gratitude suggests that focusing on and expressing gratitude will boost our sense of happiness and well-being both in the short term and over time.[13] In addition, generating feelings of gratitude can actually help us learn better, be more creative at solving problems, and even become more intuitive. I also find that gratitude strengthens my faith and trust in the Lord as I tune into His blessings and love.

A few years ago I realized I was getting repetitive with my prayers, regenerating the same list of concerns every night and morning. I decided instead to put my long, concentrated "Heavenly-Father-I-really-need-to-talk-to-you" prayers at the beginning of the day, then at the end of the day to pray only gratitude. At night I tell Heavenly Father about the little delights or major blessings I think were wonderful that day, things I really appreciated and enjoyed. Then I go to sleep with a peaceful heart. For months at a time I simply told God each night about my favorite part of the day. Other times I've looked for the happy surprise in each day, of which there is always at least one (to my happy surprise). Sometimes I have focused on remembering people who have helped me, or I've listed three new things I'm grateful for from the day.

Look for the happy surprises in each day.

We don't need to wait for night to fall to feel grateful, of course. Any time we need a change of perspective, a bit of hope in a dark hour, or a boost to our mood, focusing on gratitude can help. Gratitude not only puts us on the path to happiness, it actually begins to change our physiology, the way our heart rate works, and how our brain functions. An extra question that will deepen your gratitude further is to ask yourself why this positive thing you're grateful for came about. What allowed that good thing to come into your life? Was it the result of another person's effort? If so, then you can feel your connection to a world bigger than yourself. Was it because you simply showed up? If so, then you can feel rewarded for your effort and risk to try. Was it because Heavenly Father is gracious even when we are grumpy? If so, then you can allow your faith in His goodness to grow. Was it because you were looking for and receptive to something to be grateful for? If so, then you can remember to be more open in the future as well.

It is amazing to contemplate how many people are involved in something as simple as your evening meal—all the people who worked in fields, drove trucks and plows, made packages and equipment, shared skills and talents, stocked shelves or staffed cash registers, cut, diced, cooked, stored, planned, risked, and loved so that you could eat today. Such reflections also deepen our gratitude.

Focusing on gratitude can help our children be

more aware of the goodness in their lives as well. A fun nightly ritual is to ask each person about his or her favorite part of the day, or to think through together what had to happen and who had to help to bring some good thing into their lives.

Researchers at the Institute of Heartmath (heart-math.org) have discovered that gratitude is the easiest positive emotion for us to generate at will, and that doing so changes the way our hearts and minds operate. They have developed simple training equipment and exercises to help people use the natural rhythms of the heart to reduce stress and improve well-being.

Are you game to try one? Here it is:

1. Think of a problem you're experiencing these days that is on your mind a lot. Describe that problem in a sentence.

_____

_____

2. What feelings come up for you when you think about this problem? List several.

_____

_____

3. Now do this next step before you read further: close your eyes for one to two minutes (that's actually a pretty long time) and concentrate on creating the feeling of gratitude in your body. In other words, don't just make a mental list of things you are grateful for, but try to actually let that list sink into your heart and body. Do whatever it takes to actually generate the feeling of gratitude, and then try to stay in that feeling for one or two minutes. Try this now.

4. Basking in that feeling of gratitude, think about the problem that you are facing. Allow the feeling of gratitude to surround that problem, and notice if any ideas come to mind as to how you might approach the problem. If nothing comes to mind, just continue to generate feelings of gratitude for another minute or two. If something does come to mind, write it down.

_____

_____

5. Whether or not something came to mind about your problem, what feelings are you noticing now? Write them down.

_____

_____

6. Now compare the feelings you wrote for step #5 with those you wrote for step #2. Has there been a change? For most people the answer is yes. Often there is some step toward resolution or a new approach to the problem that has also come to mind, along with feelings of increased hopefulness or peace. How long did it take to get from the first list to the second? Less than two minutes. That is the power of gratitude.

So don't try to feel happy. Try to feel grateful. Gratitude is a true principle, a vital step on the path to happiness.

5. Celebrate Failure

There's a saying your mother probably taught you: If a thing is worth doing, it's worth doing well. That's valuable advice to an extent, but I'd like to suggest a revision of that old advice that I've learned to appreciate even more: If a thing is worth doing, it's worth doing badly.[14] All this means is that it is better to do something badly than to not do it at all. It's better to do something badly while we learn to do it better. It is especially important to be willing to do badly at things that are important, because anything that is really important to do well is difficult and complicated, and if we aren't willing to do such things badly, we will never learn to do them better.

For example, how many mistakes on the piano does a great musician make in a lifetime? How many grammatical errors does it take before a child becomes proficient at a language? How many math errors precede a great engineering breakthrough? How many times does a parent mess up in trying to raise a child? We have to be willing to endure a lot of mistake making, fumbles, embarrassing moments, or poor judgment calls to get to the point where we can play the piano well, speak like a native, solve a difficult problem, or build a successful relationship. Thousands of hours go into these accomplishments, and we've got to be willing to do such things badly at first or we won't ever get to the point of doing them well.

In fact, all of the most important things—praying, parenting, doing missionary work, fulfilling Church callings, choosing a career, developing talents—all of these are things we have to be willing to do clumsily at first if we're going to eventually do them better. Life itself falls into this category. We're going to do a lot of it badly.

Don't mistake me here. When I talk about celebrating failure, I'm not talking about sin. Willful rebellion against God is nothing to celebrate! Don't forget the first half of your mother's maxim: "If a thing is worth doing . . ." Sin never falls in that category, and we need to be constantly on guard against temptation and the adversary's claims that sin doesn't really matter.

Nor do I want to suggest that we should be *satisfied* with doing things badly. The only reason to celebrate failures is when we can view them as stepping stones on the climb to greater achievements. We can celebrate the risks we're taking along the way to getting things right—risks that we can afford to take because of the Atonement of Jesus Christ. When it comes to our attempts to progress, faltering though they may be, a key message of the Atonement is: "Do things badly, get better at them, learn, grow, try again, and I will cover your losses." Being willing to do things badly is a very important mind-set.

I forget this lesson regularly, especially when I think I'm about to do something I really care about. I was recently asked to give a talk on the Atonement for a Relief Society gathering in my stake. There is no topic I feel more reverence for, and few groups of people I would want more to do right by. So I read and studied, prayed and fasted, trying to prepare to write the best talk I could for this occasion. I got nowhere. Everything I wrote felt like drivel. The closer the time came, the more desperate I felt. As I lay in bed one night pleading for help, the reminder came: *If this talk is worth doing, it is worth doing badly. You can't write a good talk until you are willing to write a bad one. Start there.*

I got it. The next day I started with the really mediocre talk pieces I'd thrown out once, then worked on them a little at a time until they got better, rather than waiting for the stroke of inspiration that would solve my problem and inspire my confidence. I don't know that I ended up with a great talk, but I ended up with a good talk, a good enough talk for the Spirit to use in positive ways. But I didn't start with a good talk, and I couldn't write a good talk until I was willing to start with a bad one.

Competence requires not only time and effort but risk and resilience. That is an idea worth spreading. Another little nightly ritual to try with your friends or your family is to ask, "Who had a great failure today?" How crucial it is that we praise ourselves and one another for the important risks we took, the efforts we made even when they didn't pan out, or the failures we brushed ourselves off from, getting up to try again. Failure is not the end of the world but the beginning of growth and learning. We can model that belief for others when we celebrate failure, saying: "How great that you tried out for that part even though you didn't get it." "I'm so proud of you for making the effort to befriend that person even if they didn't respond." "I'm so glad you studied hard for that test even though you didn't get the A that you wanted." "When you keep working like that, you are going to improve and grow so much."

In fact, praising effort is a better motivator for children or employees than praising intelligence or raw talent.[15] When we overdo telling people they're smart, they may start to shy away from exposing their ignorance or weaknesses so as to protect their image from being tarnished. They may start to see intelligence as a mysterious trait people have or don't have rather than something to cultivate and explore. They may fear letting others see the ways they aren't smart, so they don't tend to take as many risks or ask as many questions, feeling ashamed of their ignorance. But when we point out how hard someone works, then hard work becomes core to their identity, and hard work is something that is always in their control.

Think about a time when you experienced a really big failure, a time when you were deeply disappointed, made a terrible choice, or in some other way took a big risk that ended badly. In a sentence or two, what happened?

_____

_____

Now ask yourself, "What did I learn from that experience that changed my life for the better?" Give yourself time to reflect on that question, then write your answers.

_____

_____

Finally, ask yourself what you feel best about in how you handled that difficult situation or its aftermath. What values were you true to despite your regrets?

_____

_____

I would be willing to bet that some of the most important lessons of your life show up in your answers to those questions. Failure is not an end in itself. It is a great teacher, if we are willing to be humble, correct our mistakes when we can, and allow the perspective-changing lessons we learn to sink deep into our hearts. When we fail, it is as if the Lord puts our feet to the fire of sanctification and says, "This is what we're here for, to discover together what can happen next when it feels like all is lost. Now what? How are you going to handle this? What can you learn? Will you still trust me to love and redeem you?"

Yes, being willing to do things badly, take the risk of failing, and rejoice in the chance to learn and practice resilience is a sure step on the path of happiness.

6. Don't Try to Get Help with Your Problems

If you want to get happier, don't try to get help with your problems. Don't turn to therapy for answers. And yes, I'm a therapist, so let me explain what I mean. Therapy might help you get out of misery and back to neutral; it just isn't great for getting you to the positive side of the scale. Don't get me wrong—neutral is a lot better than miserable, and therapy can be a wonderful help when we're injured or miserable. Therapy just isn't intended to help us get happy.

While turning to others to help us be happier is not a very successful approach, offering help to others is. A proven habit of happiness that people can use

Remember to help somebody today.

to boost their feelings of well-being is to help somebody else.[16]

A young woman gave a talk in our stake conference a few years ago that really impressed me. She said that for years as she left for school her mother said to her, "Remember to help somebody today." When she returned home, her mother would ask her, "Who did you help today?" The young woman, who seemed unusually confident, mature, and happy, added, "I don't report to my mother anymore, but I still try to help somebody every day, and I report to the Lord."

My husband regularly includes in his prayers a request to be aware of how he can be useful to those who might need help. He has many sweet spiritual promptings and connecting experiences as those prayers are answered. I seldom see him feel overwhelmed by these promptings, which seem to take into account his own needs and schedule as well as those of others. He is a happier person because of his desire and willingness to help those around him in small, unobtrusive ways.

Of course, there are times when we are the ones who need help, just as there are times when we have given enough and need to stop. Asking the Lord who we can help today is partly about recognizing the good we already do and tuning into the blessings we already have—not loading ourselves down with more giving than we can handle. If we tend to be "human doings" instead of "human beings," we may need counsel from other people to help us not "run faster than [we have] strength," which, the scriptures caution us, is "not requisite" (Mosiah 4:27).

Who have you helped so far today? What did you do to help?

_____

_____

Don't skip over this question. Spend a moment really thinking about how the work you've done so far today or the efforts you've made are connected to blessing other people. Admittedly, sometimes I honestly can't think of a single thing I did to help anybody that day. But reflecting on this question often not only redirects my behavior, it helps me see my existing behavior in a new light. A happier light.

7. Don't Endure to the End

Don't endure to the end? How can that be a good idea?

I love President Gordon B. Hinckley's statement, "Life is to be enjoyed, not just endured." Ah. So how can I truly enjoy, not just endure, to the end? For openers, I can regularly make a list of ten tiny delights costing little or nothing that would help me truly receive the goodness already in my life a little more fully. Here's my list for today:

- Go outside and take in the sunset
- Really look at my granddaughter's smile
- Put clean sheets on the bed
- Make homemade soup and bread to share

- Buy a new missionary her suitcase
- Plan a woodworking project for a gift
- Go to the pet store and pet the rabbits
- Drop in on a friend
- Clear a name for temple work
- Put on perfume

Okay, your turn: note ten little things that would add a little enjoyment and delight to your life or someone else's.

_____

_____

I have a friend who dreams of winning the lottery so he can buy a boat, a motorcycle, and a big house. But while we tend to remember a big purchase and the big boost of pleasure we felt in it, that pleasure is generally short-lived. Research suggests we would actually be happier spending a little of our money at a time on relatively small things that bring us delight, spending it on experiences we share with others, and especially spending it on other people, rather than spending it on big-ticket items we seldom use or don't really need.[17] Of course, if you do come into a whole slew of money, pay off the mortgage and replace your broken-down car. But portion out some of it to spend on an occasional ice cream in the summer, a hayride with friends in the fall, warm gloves to give a homeless person in winter, and hyacinths for your daughter in spring. Having a sense of abundance—enough and to spare of what matters most—is not about how much more we are given, but about how much we give away and how much we truly *receive* what we already have.

My mother died a few years ago after a long battle with Alzheimer's disease. For the last few years of her life she didn't always remember who I was, but she did always notice and thank the people who helped her. She always commented on the beauty of the clouds. She enjoyed the taste of good chocolate or a ripe peach. She marveled at the beauty of fall leaves. Those tiny pleasures of connection and delight were all that was left to her in the end, but the way she appreciated and savored such things still reminds me to "enjoy to the end."

A New List

Let's rewrite our list of happy habits in a little more positive light:

1. Put more energy into contributing to the world from your strengths than into overcoming weaknesses

2. Build an exercise routine (or any positive routine) by starting small, letting motivation grow from consistent but unobjectionably small actions

3. Invest in learning and practicing the skills of friendship: making and receiving bids; managing conflict with calm, curiosity, and compassion; celebrating success; and making room for individual differences.

4. Regularly generate and express feelings of gratitude.

5. Take the risk to do important things, even when it means doing them badly at first.

6. Help someone else every day.

7. Make time to enjoy little pleasures that don't take a lot of money, buy experiences more than things, and spend money on others.

There you have it: enough habits of happiness to keep you smiling for months! You've made some good lists and thought of some good places to start. Now pick just one—the one that sounds the most fun or interesting—and begin to make it a part of your daily life for the next few weeks. When that one starts to lose its glitter, add or switch to another. Cycle through them over the next year, and notice that even though your problems don't disappear, your children don't become perfect, your job doesn't get easier, or your questions don't all get answered, your footing on the path to happiness is a little more sure, you are a little closer to living your truest values, and the Spirit of Truth is a little more obvious in your life.

As for me, I'm going to go change my sheets. Or maybe I'll put on my exercise clothes, just because they're *comfortable*!

Notes

1. Actually this offer eventually fell through, but he did get $1.5 million. See Martin E. P. Seligman (2011), *Flourish: A Visionary New Understanding of Happiness and Well-Being* (New York: Free Press), 7–8.

2. Seligman (2011), 37–38.

3. C. Peterson and M.E.P. Seligman (2003), eds., *The VIA Classification of Strengths and Virtues* (Washington, DC: American Psychological Association).

4. M. E. P. Seligman, T. A. Steen, N. Park, and C. Peterson (2005), "Positive psychology progress: empirical validation of interventions," *American Psychologist, 60,* 410–21.

5. Ibid.

6. J. A. Blumenthal et al. (1999), "Effects of exercise training

on older patients with major depression," *Archives of Internal Medicine, 159 (19),* 2349–2356.

7. For a review of possible explanations of this phenomenon, see S. S. Wang (2013), "Hard-wired to hate exercise?" *Wall Street Journal,* February 19, 2013, U.S. online edition.

8. For this and other great ideas on how to stop procrastinating, see D. D. Burns (1989), *The Feeling Good Handbook: Using the New Mood Therapy in Everyday Life* (New York: William Morrow and Co.), 169–206.

9. See "Item 10: I have a best friend at work," *Gallup Business Journal,* May 26, 1999.

10. J. M. Gottman (2002), *The Relationship Cure* (New York: Random House).

11. J. M. Gottman and N. Silver (1999), *The Seven Principles for Making Marriage Work* (New York: Three Rivers Press).

12. S.I. Gable, H. T. Reis, E. A. Impett, and E. R. Asher (2004), "What do you do when things go right? The intrapersonal and interpersonal benefits of sharing positive events," *Journal of Personality and Social Psychology 87,* 228–45.

13. Seligman, Steen, Park, and Peterson (2005), 410–21.

14. An idea expressed by many, including J. Cameron

(1992), *The Artist's Way: A Spiritual Path to Higher Creativity* (Los Angeles: Jeremy Tarcher).

15. E. A. Gunderson et al. (2013), "Parent praise to 1–3 year olds predicts children's motivational frameworks five years later," *Child Development,* online version.

16. C. E. Jenkinson et al. (2013), "Is volunteering a public health intervention? A systematic review and meta-analysis of the health and survival of volunteers," *BMC Public Health 13,*773.

17. E. W. Dunn and M. Norton (2013). *Happy Money: The Science of Smarter Spending* (New York: Simon & Schuster).